Kombucha Recipes: Fermented Tea and Drinks for Beginners

How to Make Kombucha at Home – Simple and Easy!

TABLE OF CONTENTS

Introduction 1

Getting to Know Kombucha 2

The History of Kombucha 6

What Kombucha Does to You 9

Nutritional Value 13

Essential Ingredients and Supplies 16

Different Brewing Methods 26

Delicious Kombucha Recipes 28

Troubleshooting Your Kombucha 36

Clarifying Kombucha Myths 39

Conclusion 42

Introduction

I want to thank you and congratulate you for purchasing this book.

This book contains information about kombucha: what it is, where it started, how to prepare, health benefits, and other details about kombucha you wouldn't want to miss.

This book is all about kombucha (pronounced kom-BOO-cha): what is it, what ingredients are needed to make it, how to choose the ingredients and equipment, how to brew kombucha, and what benefits are in store for you upon drinking it.

Tried to make kombucha once but failed? This book also gives you troubleshooting steps – telling you what could have gone wrong, and what you can do to fix it.

Upon reading this book, you'll realize why it suddenly became a hit in western countries after being widely popular on the other side of the world. It'll also separate the myths from the truths surrounding kombucha.

This book is for you, dear reader. You're sure to enjoy this book regardless if you're someone who has never seen or tasted kombucha his or her entire life, or someone who's an expert in making kombucha. This can serve as a handy guide, and can even help you try out new recipes too.

Lately i've become passionate about healthy living and that's when kobucha appeared. I've done lot's of research on the topic and i would like to bring my knowledge over to you through this book.

Thanks again for purchasing this book, I hope you enjoy it!

Getting to Know Kombucha

A lot of people nowadays are buzzing over kombucha, a probiotic tea, and attesting to the benefits it can give them. Apparently a fermented tea made with something weird-looking floating on top can give people the energy and immune boost they've always wanted.

Find out the truth behind the buzz – get to know kombucha.

WHAT IS KOMBUCHA?

Kombucha – a mix of bacteria (also known as SCOBY), tea and sugar – is a health drink produced by fermenting tea. This probiotic drink actually has been around for a thousand years, and is believed to provide various health benefits such as less stress, improved digestion and more energy, to name a few.

Image from Livestrong.com

There are people appalled by kombucha because of its vinegar-like smell as well as its 'one-of-a-kind' taste (there are those who say it tastes like rotten apples, while some link its taste to a cross between champagne and apple cider).

Creative kombucha makers, on the other hand, have tried making kombucha with fruit, herbs or vegetable flavors. Some do this to better motivate people in drinking kombucha, while some aim to mix in more benefits to the drink.

How Is Kombucha Made

Kombucha is at first a sugary tea, and then fermented with the help of cultured bacteria called SCOBY – Symbiotic Culture of Bacteria and Yeast. The tea is prepared, made sweet, and then the SCOBY is placed on top for the fermentation process.

A few days will pass – typically around 7 to 10 days – and after which, you can perform a taste test and see if the taste and aroma of the kombucha suits to your liking. You'll then take out the SCOBY, and store the finished kombucha for consumption.

Kombucha is sold commercially, but today, you'll learn how to make it inside your own home. All you need are simple ingredients and equipment (most of them you can find inside your kitchen pantry); as long as you follow instructions, then you'll do fine.

(Recipes of kombucha itself as well as recipes with other ingredients can be found on later chapters.)

Who Is Kombucha for?

You can drink kombucha if you're in good health, and if you're not dealing with any sickness at the moment. If you're facing any kind of health concern, then it's best to check first with your doctor to avoid any form of complications.

The following individuals should take note of the following reminders when drinking kombucha:

Children under 6 years – They have fragile bodies and are still growing; their bodies aren't ready yet to process supplements that adults drink. Contrary to its effect on adults, kombucha may end up having an effect on the child's immune system.

Children over 6 years – Children at this age may be able to drink kombucha, but only in small amounts, and preferably diluted with iced tea, water or fruit juice.

Diabetics – Diabetics can drink kombucha provided it has low sugar content. The sugars in kombucha are converted into different components as it's being fermented, but a bit of sugar still remains in the finished product.

Recovering Alcoholics – This actually varies; some love drinking kombucha because it somehow removes their desire for alcohol even with its very low alcohol content. Some, on the other hand, don't drink because even a small amount can cause negative effects on their body.

Pregnant and lactating mothers – As mentioned above, kombucha may cause harm to infants and toddlers, so mothers, both pregnant and breastfeeding, should avoid drinking kombucha as they may be able to pass it on to their unborn and infant children, respectively.

Again, don't brew kombucha if you have any health concerns that may come into conflict with it. Consult with a health professional to ensure your safety.

The Drinking Process

Like any other new substance, kombucha should only be drunk in amounts agreeable to the body when taken for the first time. For the first three to four days, you should only drink a single glass.

You can increase your intake as each day passes – the intake can reach as much as 300mL. Once the first week had passed, then you can drink the full amount of 450mL or around 12oz.

Take note that the aforementioned recommendation is only ideal for someone with good health i.e. not experiencing any health concerns. Should you have any preexisting health conditions, then your intake must be less than the mentioned levels, or better yet, be approved first by a health professional.

The History of Kombucha

It seems like kombucha is just a new trend that made its way to grocery store shelves, but kombucha has actually been present for numerous centuries. No one can really state where and when kombucha started, but various stories have been told, narrating where and when kombucha could have originated and developed.

China, Japan & Korea

Some say that it started in China and has been a drink there for two thousand years. There are records that indicate kombucha coming from China during the Qin dynasty in 221 BC and has been referred to as "The Tea of Immortality", stating that kombucha had magical powers and can help people live forever.

In Chinese, kombucha is referred to as *hongchagu* 红茶菇 ("black tea mushroom"), *chameijun* 茶霉菌 ("tea mold") or *hongchajun* 红茶菌 (lit. "black tea fungus/mushroom").

In 415 AD, the name 'kombucha' is said to have come from Japan. In Korea, a physician named 'Kombu' or 'Kambu' had given Emperor Inyko with this tea, and called it as 'kombu (his name) plus cha (tea)'.

Russia and other European Countries

Another recorded history of kombucha started in Ukraine and Russia around late 19th century. In Russia, the culture in kombucha is known as *čajnyj grib чайный гриб* (or "tea mushroom"), while the kombucha tea itself is called *квас* (tea kvass), *grib гриб* ("mushroom") or simply kvass.

Russia had this tradition of drinking 'Tea Kvass' as it was believed as a healing drink. From Russia, it had traveled to Poland, Prussia, Denmark and Germany, and had seemed to 'die' during World War II.

After the war, there was a renewed interest in kombucha through Dr. Rudolph Skelnar; the said doctor had used kombucha to treat metabolic disorders, cancers, diabetes and high blood pressure.

During the earlier parts of the 20th century, there was a hunt for cancer cure. As the scientists and data were checked by Russian scientists, they discovered that there were people who were almost cancer-free; the scientists found out that these people were drinking 'tea kvass' i.e. kombucha.

Kombucha around the World

Just for fun, get to know how kombucha is known at different parts of the world.

English – kombucha

Japanese - *kōcha kinoko* (紅茶キノコ)

Korean - *hongchabeoseotcha* (홍차버섯차)

Chinese - *chájūn* (茶菌)

Russian - *chaynyy grib* (чайный гриб)

Vietnamese - *giam tra* (giấm trà)

As you can see, kombucha is more than just a hype – it's a powerful drink that has been present for thousands of years. It has been around in different countries around the world, and people have testified and supported its health benefits.

People have sworn to experience the benefits of kombucha and attest to how it had treated them. Want to know what perks you can get out of drinking kombucha? Read the next chapter to see some of the benefits that kombucha can provide.

What Kombucha Does to You

The Chinese has referred to kombucha as the 'Immortal Health Elixir' simply because of its impressive record of benefits in treating various diseases. Kombucha may not be a miracle or a cure-all drink, but it has definitely started getting attention from the other parts of the world.

If you are one of those who aren't too familiar with this sweet tea and it's SCOBY, then read on.

KOMBUCHA HEALTH BENEFITS

Get to know the health benefits given by kombucha, and see why people are flocking to this probiotic drink.

Boosts the Immune System

Kombucha boosts your immune system well; it's rich in antioxidants that help protect your immune system. It helps control the free radicals found inside the body through various antioxidant measures.

Powerful antioxidants such as *D-saccharic acid-1, 4-lactone* (DSL) were found during fermentation, and these help support the immune-boosting capability of kombucha.

Kombucha may not affect your immune system directly, but the effects it gives to the other parts of your body help contribute to strengthen your immune system. What it does is to support the body and help the immune system perform at its optimum level.

Joint Care

Kombucha takes care of your joints through its glucosamines. Glucosamines boost one's production of synovial hyaluronic acid, which helps in preventing arthritic pain and preserving the cartilage structure.

The relief provided by kombucha is somehow similar to the relief given by NSAIDs i.e. pain relievers; it helps you minimize the medicine intake caused by joint pain.

Aside from helping support joint collagen, glucosamine-loaded kombucha also helps the collagen of the whole body and lessens wrinkle appearance on your skin.

Helps Digestion and Gut Health

Kombucha is naturally fermented with yeast and bacteria, hence it's believed to contain enzymes, probiotics, and other acids beneficial for one's digestive health. Plus, it contains good bacteria that your gut needs.

Research shows that kombucha has this ability to avoid and heal stomach ulcers and leaky guts. It can even stop candida yeast from becoming overpopulated through its live probiotic cultures; doing so gives back the balance of your digestive system.

Aside from improved digestion, the other benefits of kombucha include mental clarity and mood stability. It can also reduce or completely eliminate symptoms of internal concerns such as anxiety, depression and fibromyalgia.

Gives You Energy

Drinking kombucha tea can invigorate you and give you energy; this is because of the iron formation released from the tea during fermentation. A small amount of caffeine is also found in kombucha, together with B-vitamins that are also known to energize the body.

Kombucha helps provide energy to regular kombucha drinkers through a process called *chelation*; in this process, the iron given by kombucha helps hemoglobin improve the body's oxygen supply and boost the energy-producing process.

Helps Prevent Cancer

Kombucha is also believed to work with cancer prevention and recovery because of glucaric acid.

Even Ronald Reagan was known to drink kombucha when he was ill with cancer. At that time, chemotherapies for bladder and colon were known as treatment methods, however Reagan wasn't too comfortable with them. His physicians then obtained kombucha from Japan for Reagan to take.

Reagan was known to take a liter of kombucha daily; soon, news about his cancer wasn't read anymore. Reagan continued to drink kombucha for the rest of his days until he passed away in 2004, not because of cancer, but because of old age.

Detoxification

Kombucha has a powerful detoxifying capability. Aside from giving you a healthy liver, detoxifying also helps you steer clear of cancer. Kombucha helps detoxify your body by producing the enzymes and bacteria needed to cleanse your system, giving your pancreas less load.

Kombucha also decreases the burden of your liver; it's high in glucaric acid, an acid that helps the liver with its natural detoxification. Studies show that kombucha helps protect the liver cells from oxidative injuries, and even helped them maintain their physiology regardless of being exposed to toxins.

As you can see, there are lots of benefits that come from drinking kombucha. To first-timers, the taste may repulse or startle you, but just remember these benefits – surely they'll motivate you to at least try them out.

ANY SIDE EFFECTS?

Most people who drink kombucha don't experience any negative side effects. Kombucha is basically safe enough to drink, and is believed to bring a lot of benefits to the drinker.

Those who are easily affected include those with digestive problems as well as those with compromised immune systems. Kombucha can be acidic, so this can affect those with digestive issues such as heartburn, stomach ulcers or those with bodies that react with acidic foods.

People who have a weak immune system e.g. those affected by HIV/AIDS have to be careful in drinking kombucha – the yeast can produce bacteria that can cause sickness to the individual. Since tea is also a common allergen, then those who are sensitive to tea must be careful regarding their kombucha intake.

Of course, it all boils down to you trusting your body, and relying on it to tell you how it reacts. If it reacts negatively upon drinking kombucha, then stop for a while, and observe. To be on the safe side, check first with a medical professional to avoid any complications.

Nutritional Value

To further support the claim that kombucha is indeed a healthy drink to consume, here's a list of the nutrients found in kombucha.

Vitamins and Minerals

Here is a list of vitamins and minerals believed to be found in kombucha.

Thiamine (Vitamin B1) – This helps in preventing atherosclerosis, skin aging, brain cell aging, arthritic conditions, free radical damage, cancer, and weakened immune systems.

Riboflavin (Vitamin B2) – Properties of riboflavin help prevent arthritic condition and certain allergies.

Niacin (Vitamin B3) – Niacin helps skin tissues heal faster and prevent free radical damage.

Pyridoxine (Vitamin B6) – This helps prevent rheumatism, obesity, atherosclerosis, strokes and free radical damage.

Folic Acid / Folate (Vitamin B9) – This helps the body make new cells; it reduces homocysteine through the help of Vitamin B12.

Cobalamin (Vitamin B12) – Vitamin B12 helps with one's sense of wellbeing, plus helps with making people remember.

L-ascorbic Acid (Vitamin C) – This vitamin is essential for one's normal growth and development. It's also said to play a great role in one's immune system.

Probiotics

Kombucha has beneficial yeasts and bacteria that help suppress or eliminate yeast, parasites and harmful bacteria. Hence, those who have candida issues may be able to drink kombucha.

Probiotics help support one's digestive tract and assist with common digestive issues e.g. diarrhea, constipation, inflammatory bowel disease and irritable bowel syndrome.

It's important to deal with digestive health issues because proper digestion can lead to effective absorption of nutrients that help nourish and treat the body, leading the way to a better overall health.

Antioxidants

Kombucha is a recommended drink because of its antioxidants, known for helping lessen inflammation, fight free radicals, and reduce the oxidative damage to one's DNA.

The antioxidants in kombucha include vitamin C, vitamin E, glucaric acid (D-saccharic acid), beta carotene and other carotenoids. It also includes polyphenols and compounds that contain antioxidant capabilities.

Because of the fermentation process, the antioxidant levels are higher compared to simple tea – the vitamin C levels are 100 times higher, while vitamin E levels are 25 times higher.

Energy Boosters

Aside from the B-vitamins mentioned that are found in kombucha, it also contains other energy boosters such as iron and a bit of caffeine.

You'll increase your energy levels and have better concentration – the energy levels you attain isn't the kind that you get from caffeine or sugar rush. The energy kombucha provides does not solely come from sugar and caffeine, that's why you don't experience any crashes.

Plus, kombucha can help your body extract bigger amounts of energy from your food intake.

Essential Ingredients and Supplies

To make kombucha tea, five ingredients are often stated: tea, water, starter tea, sugar and SCOBY. Every component is important to produce kombucha tea of the best quality that's why you have to choose each of them properly.

INGREDIENTS NEEDED FOR MAKING KOMBUCHA

What ingredients do you need to make kombucha?

Tea

Tea is an important ingredient for fermenting kombucha. Real tea (*Camellia sinensis*) will work better compared to herbal tea due to its minerals as well as nitrogen; kombucha may also react to various aromatic oils found in various teas. To avoid chemical contaminants, choose organic tea as much as possible.

Kinds of Tea for Kombucha

Here are the kinds of tea that you can use for kombucha:

Green Tea – To prevent oxidation, withered green tea will either be heated or steamed, and afterwards rolled and dried. Green tea has this light green color and a delicate taste. Sencha, a kind of Japanese tea, will produce a fine kombucha.

Black Tea – Black tea is created from fully fermented leaves. To produce this tea, the leaves are spread out and allowed to wilt on its own before being fired, giving a deep, rich flavor plus an amber brew.

Oolong Tea – A cross between green and black tea in appearance and in taste, oolong tea is gently rolled after picking, and then made to partially ferment until the leaves' edge turn brown.

White Tea – White tea is one of the least common and most delicate variants of tea; they are plucked 48 hours at most between the buds become mature and when they open. White tea has retained its antioxidant properties due to it not being steamed or rolled unlike green and black teas but air dried instead.

The tea type you choose can affect not only your SCOBY health but also your finished product's taste, so you have to pick out your tea carefully.

Teas are believed to have less amounts of caffeine compared to coffee; if you're really concerned about your caffeine intake, then you can go for decaffeinated teas instead.

Water

You'd think choosing water is easy, but it's not; you still have to consider different factors in picking out what water to choose.

The water you'd be using should be as contaminant-free as possible. You can just use basic, inexpensive spring water; filtered water is more recommended so that you can remove chemicals, contaminants and other additives.

If you can't filter the water, then you can just aerate or boil it to remove the chlorine. Chlorine may also evaporate if you let the water stand for 24 hours.

You don't have to choose water with high mineral content; water with mineral contents that are too high may end up harming the SCOBY. Alkalized, structured or pH-adjusted water isn't also appropriate for kombucha.

Sugar

As much as you may like your drinks to be as healthy as possible, you can't eliminate sugar because you need it for the fermentation process. You can't substitute or bypass sugar; you can't even use less sugar because it'll starve your SCOBY.

The longer you ferment your kombucha, the less amount of sugar will remain. To achieve the best balance between flavor and sugar, brew your kombucha from 7 to 30 days.

Which Sugar Is Ideal for Kombucha?

Is the sugar you're using ideal for kombucha? Check out these kinds of sugar to see if it's a good match for kombucha.

Ideal for Kombucha

White cane sugar – This is good for brewing kombucha because it's pure and is free of minerals.

Organic cane juice crystals – This kind of sugar has very low mineral content; it's white but unbleached. Hence, this is also an ideal sugar for making kombucha.

Not Ideal for Kombucha

Whole cane, brown, or raw sugars – These are less refined sugars that contain molasses. Sugars like these aren't recommended for kombucha because they're hard on the SCOBY – using these will end up producing a yeasty kombucha and may shorten your SCOBY's life.

Agave, coconut, maple, palm syrups or sugars – These sugars are taken from different plants; the results you'll get from using them are somehow inconsistent, hence not recommended for kombucha.

Honey – Honey is produced by bees; it's often raw or pasteurized. Results also vary when used; when using honey, have a spare SCOBY with you. Honey's not usually recommended, though, because its antimicrobial properties may end up harming the SCOBY.

Xylitol, stevia and other artificial sweeteners – These are the most common sugar substitutes; they don't have the right nutrients necessary for fermenting SCOBY, hence not recommended for kombucha.

Starter Tea

The 'starter tea' refers to the acidic liquid added to the kombucha that you're currently brewing. This is an important part of the process: adding the starter tea is important not only to the SCOBY itself but also to the entire batch of kombucha.

The most recommended starter tea to use is a properly brewed and unflavored kombucha tea made during your previous batch.

What if you don't have starter tea on hand? Here are some options you can try out:

You can try to use white distilled vinegar; it can provide the portion of the acidic liquid required for brewing a kombucha batch.

You can also buy raw and unflavored kombucha tea from the store.

Using starter tea for your kombucha can also help control the brew's pH levels that's why it's an important component for brewing.

SCOBY

The SCOBY, as previously mentioned a few times already in this book, is an important component in making kombucha. It's the kombucha culture that somehow looks like a chunky pancake, and is often referred to as a mushroom, or the "mother".

To have a SCOBY of your own, you have several options:

You can directly buy your own SCOBY from various stores, usually online, and will often be given to you in a dehydrated state with instructions on how to activate it.

Do you know someone who makes kombucha? He or she usually has a spare SCOBY to share, plus around ½ cup of starter tea. This should be good enough for your first kombucha batch.

You can also check kombucha fermenting groups in your area; they can serve as a good source of SCOBY.

You can make your own SCOBY from scratch by combining sugar, tea and pre-made kombucha.

Yes, it's safe to make your own kombucha from scratch, as long as you follow the instructions well and keep the kombucha clean as it's being fermented. If you think something has gone wrong, then don't hesitate to throw the batch away and make a new one.

Making Your Own SCOBY

Here's how you can make your own SCOBY from scratch.

First, prepare the tea wherein you'll be growing your SCOBY.

You can either buy pre-made unflavored kombucha, or make a cup of green or black tea.

If you chose to prepare black or green tea, then while the water is still hot, add 1 to 2 tablespoons of white sugar. Mix sugar until thoroughly dissolved, then cool the mixture until it reaches room temperature.

Combine the cooled tea and raw kombucha in a single jar, and cover the jar using a paper coffee filter or tightweave dish towel. Secure the cover using a tight rubber band.

Start the fermentation by placing the tea in a warm spot (make sure it's out of direct sunlight) in about 7 days.

You should see a baby SCOBY starting to develop after a week. It'll start off as a clear jelly or blob; soon, it'll be less translucent, thicker, and whiter as time passes. (*If you don't see any development after 3 weeks, then throw it away and start over.*)

Wait for the SCOBY to "grow" at least ¼ inch thick before using it for your first batch of kombucha tea; this part may take up to 30 days.

Once you're done, keep the kombucha tea and your newly-grown SCOBY for your future kombucha batches.

You're done! You have made your own SCOBY for making your own kombucha tea. Check out other recipes found in this book to concoct kombucha that fits your taste.

EQUIPMENT FOR MAKING KOMBUCHA

Aside from choosing the right ingredients, you also have to make sure you're using the right equipment. This is to ensure that you'll be producing kombucha of the best quality. All you need are these supplies: a brewing container plus a cover.

Brewing Container

In choosing a brewing container, you should pick out those that are made of the following materials:

Ceramic – When choosing ceramic containers, make sure the glaze of the container is food-grade to avoid any possible contact with lead.

Porcelain – Porcelain containers are safe for brewing kombucha, provided they are food-grade containers. Those that aren't food grade e.g. decorative pottery and vases should not be used.

Glass – Glass containers are the best option for making kombucha; glass won't react to the brew's acidity, plus they don't contain chemicals and don't scratch easily. Plus, glass containers are simple and inexpensive to obtain.

On the other hand, avoid these kinds of containers:

Crystal – Crystal containers have lead, hence they are not ideal for brewing kombucha.

Plastic – Plastic containers should not be used as they can be easily damaged; scratches can easily accumulate foreign bacteria. Even food-grade plastic containers can end up being harmful to the SCOBY.

Metal – Metal containers destroy kombucha; they should not be used except for when the container is made of stainless steel. Some believe stainless steel containers can be an Acceptable alternative – they aren't totally recommended, but some have used stainless steel containers and have succeeded in doing so.

Covers for Brewing Kombucha

It's important to cover fermenting kombucha as they can easily attract critters such as fruit flies. To keep these critters out, cover your container; covering it will protect both the SCOBY and the kombucha itself.

An excellent choice for a kombucha cover is a *tight-weave dish towel* or a *coffee filter* secured using a rubber band. Don't use screens or loose-weave fabrics because these will defeat the purpose of covering the kombucha and still attract ants and fruit flies.

As much as you'd like to use a tight lid, don't do so – your kombucha needs enough airflow to ferment properly and effectively. Tight lids will restrict airflow by not allowing air to circulate, hence meddling with the brewing process.

ADDITIONAL REMINDERS

Kombucha can be brewed in containers of any size as long as it can hold all the ingredients inside and still keep the correct ratios.

Remember that the fermentation process can take 7 to 30 days; the amount of kombucha you're making should be enough to provide necessary amounts for drinking plus have enough starter tea for your future batches of kombucha.

You should also bear in mind that the surface area's size will also matter in brewing kombucha – it will somehow affect the rate of the brewing process. Case in point: kombucha stored in a container having a 9" diameter surface will brew faster compared to kombucha stored in a container having a 3" diameter surface.

Different Brewing Methods

There are two known ways of brewing kombucha: batch brewing and continuous brewing. Get to know what they are as well as their differences in this chapter.

Batch Brewing

Batch brewing is ideal for kombucha starters – those who will try kombucha for the first time and are still unsure if kombucha is really for them – or those who only wish to drink kombucha for a few glasses a week.

If you're just into drinking small amounts of kombucha, if you're unsure if you have the time to maintain your brewed tea, then go for the batch brew.

Batch brewing is done by preparing your usual tea of kombucha, and when you're done, you remove the SCOBY as well as a small amount of starter tea for your next batch. Usually there's no spare left once you're done drinking. All gone.

Those who love drinking kombucha and always wish to have a prepared brew inside their home would find batch brewing both tedious and time-consuming – you end up exerting the same efforts every time you wish to drink kombucha – and so opt to do continuous brewing instead.

Continuous Brewing

The simplest and easiest kombucha brewing method is known as 'continuous brewing'. What's good about this method is that all health benefits of the ingredients are readily available as long as you have your kombucha with you.

It's also pretty convenient and needs low maintenance – you don't have to do weekly cleaning, plus no need to worry about the SCOBY because molds won't likely form. (Of course, your SCOBY dying out and turning black is another story.)

All you do is maintain an established ferment, hence less chances of your brew being influenced by yeasts and bacteria. You can take amounts of kombucha as frequently as you like, as long as you pour an equivalent amount of tea as replacement.

To do continuous brewing, all you need is a container that can hold at least 2 gallons. The ideal fermenting temperature is around 74°F to 84°F. It's important to take note of the temperature – if your temperature is around the 60s or even lower, you'll end up fostering the wrong kinds of yeasts and bacteria. The good probiotics, on the other hand, will become dormant and ineffective.

How to Choose

Most people prefer going for the continuous method, especially once they've realized the good behind drinking kombucha. Plus, less mess and less energy exerted if you do continuous brewing.

If, on the other hand, you're always on the go and you won't have the time to maintain and drink large amounts of kombucha, plus if you don't mind spending the effort to make an entirely new batch every now and then, then you can go for batch brewing.

So which one is better? It all depends on your lifestyle and your preferences. You can go for batch brewing at first, and once your taste for kombucha has grown, then you can go for continuous brewing so you can make the most of the benefits kombucha can provide.

Delicious Kombucha Recipes

You don't have to enjoy kombucha in it's plain flavor – you can also add fruits, herbs and vegetables to make it taste better, and even healthier.

Enjoy these kombucha recipes and reap the benefits each recipe provides.

Sweet Tea Kombucha Recipe

This sweet tea kombucha recipe is naturally carbonated and is ultimately healthy with its probiotics, enzymes and acids. It's very easy to make, and costs less than store-bought kombucha.

Ingredients:

- Brewed sweetened tea, 1 gallon
- Kombucha SCOBY
- Pre-made kombucha, ½ cup

Procedure:

- Prepare the sweet tea. Add ½ cup of sugar. (Organic or regular is good, but don't use honey.)
- Allow tea to cool at room temperature. Make sure the tea has cooled down completely, because hot tea can harm your SCOBY.
- Pour cooled tea inside glass jars. Leave an inch of room. Pour the pre-made kombucha afterwards.

- Use clean hands to place the SCOBY on top of the sweet tea and kombucha mixture. Ideally, the SCOBY should float; if it doesn't, just let it sink to the bottom of the jar.
- Cover the jar using a cloth or coffee filter and secure it with rubber bands.
- Place the jar in a dark corner of your pantry. Allow to ferment for about 7 days. Test the kombucha by taking a sip using a straw. Your kombucha should taste tart but also taste slightly sweet.

Ginger Kombucha

Ginger and kombucha is a good combination; kombucha gives off a tart and fizzy taste, while ginger brings a punch that's warm and spicy.

Ingredients:

- White sugar, 1 cup
- Black tea, 4 bags
- SCOBY, 1 for every fermentation jar
- Pre-made unflavored kombucha (can be from the last kombucha you made, or store-bought)
- Water, 3 ½ quarts
- Green tea, 4 bags
- Fresh ginger, 2 to 3 inches

Equipment:

You'd also need clean soda bottles, swing-top bottles, or 6 16oz bottles plus plastic lids.

Procedure:

- First, bring water to a boil. Remove boiling water from heat, and then stir in the sugar. Let it dissolve.

- Drop in the bags of tea; allow them to steep until the water has reached room temperature. This may take a couple of hours, depending on the pot's size. Once the tea has cooled down, remove the bags of tea. Afterwards, stir in your pre-made kombucha.

- Pour your mixture of tea and pre-made kombucha into a 1-gallon glass jar. Use clean hands to gently slide the SCOBY on top of your mixture. Cover the jar's mouth with paper towels or cheesecloth, and secure it using a rubber band.

- Store the fermenting kombucha at room temperature. Make sure it's not under direct sunlight and it won't get jostled. Allow it to ferment for about 7 to 10 days; check it from time to time.

- Upon reaching its 7th day, taste the kombucha. Pour a little amount into a cup. Once it reaches that balance between tartness and sweetness, then it's ready for bottling.

- Use clean hands to gently take the SCOBY out of the kombucha, and lay it down on a clean plate. If you're considering to make a new batch of kombucha soon, then take out enough to make a starter tea, and set it aside.

- Clean the ginger well; you don't have to peel it. Grate or chop the ginger finely; catch juices that may collect. You should end up with around 1 ½ tablespoons of ginger juice and puree; divide this evenly between all the bottles.

- Pour your fermented kombucha inside bottles using a small funnel. Don't maximize the space; leave around an inch free in every bottle.

- Store the ginger kombucha at room temperature. Keep it out of direct sunlight; 1-3 days should be enough for the kombucha to carbonate. How'd you know? If you used plastic bottles, then the bottles should be solid as a rock; if you used glass, then you should open bottles every now and then to check (don't worry, it'll re-carbonate once you place the cap back).

- Once it's all carbonated, then you can refrigerate them for them to cool down, for 4 hours at least. You can keep your kombucha inside the refrigerator for a couple of weeks.

Chia Seed Kombucha

Kombucha and chia seeds are both nutritious themselves; what more if you're going to take a drink that's a combination of them?

Ingredients:

- Chia seeds, ¼ cup
- Water, 1 cup
- Kombucha, 1 cup (either store-bought or homemade)

Procedure:

- Submerge chia seeds in water. Mix well; cover afterwards.
- Keep the submerged seeds overnight inside the fridge.
- Mix in around ¼ to ½ cup of the chia gel mixture for every 1 cup of kombucha. Pour chia gel mixture based on your desired thickness.
- Mix well and enjoy.

Kombucha Margarita Mocktail

Here's an easy probiotic rich kombucha mocktail recipe that you're sure to enjoy.

Ingredients:

- Coconut water, 1 cup
- Fresh lime juice, ¼ cup
- Kombucha, 1 cup (either homemade or bought)
- Ginger, freshly grated, ½ teaspoon
- Ice, 1 cup
- Lime slices (for garnishing)

Procedure:

- Mix all ingredients inside a blender. Blend until you've reached that icy consistency.
- Pour finished mocktail into two glasses.
- Add lime garnishes; enjoy straight away.

Strawberry Kombucha

Strawberries can give kombucha a light fruity flavor. Not only it is delicious, but it's also healthy as it's packed with beneficial probiotics.

Ingredients:

- Strawberries, medium-sized, about 4 to 6 pieces
- Unflavored kombucha, 16oz, can be homemade or bought
- ½ teaspoon of sugar (optional, add according to taste)

Procedure:

- Place strawberries inside a 16 ounce vessel. Fill it up with kombucha while leaving around ½ inch of headspace. Cap the vessel tightly and store in room temperature.
- Culture the strawberry kombucha mix for about 3 to 7 days, or until kombucha is carbonated according to your preference.
- Once carbonated, store the bottles inside the refrigerator.
- When ready for drinking, open the bottle carefully to avoid kombucha from spilling.
- The strawberries can be strained or not, depending on your preference.

Kombucha Coffee

Kombucha coffee can serve as an alternative to your regular drinking coffee.

Ingredients:

- Plain coffee, freshly brewed, 2 cups
- Sugar, ½ cup
- Kombucha SCOBY

Procedure:

- Pour hot coffee inside a glass or ceramic container. Add sugar, and allow the mixture to reach room temperature. Make sure the coffee mixture has no leftover coffee grounds.
- Add the SCOBY; cover the jar afterwards using a coffee filter or a tight-weave cloth. Secure the cover using a rubber band.
- Ferment the kombucha coffee mixture in room temperature for about 7 days. Keep the mixture out of direct sunlight. After a week, take a few sips of the kombucha everyday using a straw.
- You're ready to drink the kombucha once the taste is pleasurable to you.

There you have it – 6 kombucha recipes you can try out, especially if you're just preparing kombucha for the first time. These recipes are easy enough for you to make, and will end up giving you the same benefits.

Safety Reminders

Safety has always been the primary concern of those making kombucha in their homes, and is definitely understandable. Like any other food, you should show utmost care during preparation and storage of kombucha to prevent contamination.

Just remember that in every step, your hands and utensils must be cleaned – preferably with soap and water – to ensure your kombucha won't be contaminated. Keep the cultures covered and stored inside a clean environment to lessen risks of insects and contaminants infecting your kombucha.

As long as you perform all necessary steps, then you'll do just fine, and you will be able to make your own home-brewed kombucha tea.

Troubleshooting Your Kombucha

For some, fermenting kombucha ends up being a trial-and-error session. It's an easy process to follow, but it's also just normal to not get it right the first time. That's why here are some "troubleshooting" tips you can use; maybe you can still save your kombucha.

Kombucha doesn't start to ferment.

The best method of checking the progress of your kombucha is to test its flavor and aroma. If you notice that your kombucha isn't starting the fermenting process, one possible reason could be because your starter tea isn't suitable for the concoction.

- Perhaps the tea was too hot when the SCOBY was added, hence killing it.
- Maybe the place you've stored the kombucha in is too cold; find a warmer spot.
- Perhaps there was chlorine in the water.

If, on the other hand, you didn't use starters and only used fruit, then all you need to do is stir. Nothing but stir. And just be patient – maybe the kombucha just needed some time.

Surface molds develop.

Discard both the kombucha tea and the SCOBY once you see molds have formed. You can no longer save your concoction – just throw them all away. Clean the container using vinegar, soap and water. Restart the process completely using a new SCOBY.

Mold is rare, though, and there are ways to prevent mold from forming. The pre-made kombucha added on the current kombucha is what prevents surface molding. When other ferments are present aside from the kombucha, you have to stir or shake while in open vessels – this is to prevent molds from forming by disturbing them way before they become visible.

When making the vinegar, you can stir your sugar solution until the SCOBY forms. Stirring will disturb the mother, so after that, you can just increase the acidity to avoid formation of molds.

It's not carbonated enough.

It's fun to drink kombucha – one reason is because of the fizz. There are few reasons as to your kombucha not being fizzy enough; maybe the SCOBY isn't mature enough, or maybe it's because of the tea you've used.

If it's your first time brewing kombucha, then it possibly won't be fizzy as you expected; your SCOBY may not be mature enough to achieve this effect. Take note of these:

- Don't move them inside the fridge immediately; pour the kombucha after brewing inside airtight bottles and allow them to ferment at room temperature for a few days.
- Using green tea as your starter tea can produce more carbonation compared to using black tea.

As long as you take note of those reminders, then soon, you'll be able to brew a fizzy kombucha.

Kombucha ends up too sour

When your kombucha ends up too sour, that means you've probably fermented it longer than you should. The next time you make kombucha, go for a shorter fermentation time, or taste test it sooner than you did the first time.

Another possibility is that you've stored the kombucha in a warm part of your home – it could have brewed the kombucha faster than expected.

You don't have to throw the kombucha if it's too sour for your taste, though. You can try diluting it with water or with carbonated water plus sweetener; perhaps you can still adjust the taste to your liking.

If it still fails, then your overly acidified kombucha can still be used as vinegar.

My SCOBY has turned black.

Sorry to tell you, but your SCOBY has died. It could have been contaminated, or simply worn out. It takes a long time before your SCOBY dies, and when it does, all you can do is to throw away both the tea and the SCOBY.

Remember that a black SCOBY is different from seeing brown or discolored patches; those patches are just normal as these are caused by yeast build-up from the fermentation process.

Clean the container after disposing the tea and the dead SCOBY. Afterwards, you can get a new SCOBY and start over.

Don't despair if your attempts to make kombucha failed. Again, it's just normal to deal with mistakes especially if it's your first time. What you can do instead is to take note of what happened, remember what you've done, and do better the next time.

Clarifying Kombucha Myths

Others call it simply as "mushroom tea", while some refer to it as the "elixir of life". Regardless of what you call it, kombucha definitely has a lot of promising health benefits. Not everybody has heard of it, and so, a lot of myths have surrounded it.

Today, you're bound to find out the truths behind the myths about kombucha.

Kombucha is a mushroom.

Kombucha or the SCOBY may look like a mushroom, but neither of the two is one. Kombucha is made using the SCOBY – a Symbiotic Culture Of Bacteria and Yeast. Sure, both yeasts and mushrooms are fungi, but they're not siblings – more of cousins, maybe.

The yeast and bacteria create a cellulose structure where they live together; what the yeast does is to ferment the nutrient solution, creating the alcohol, which the bacteria will then convert to healthy acids helping the body.

It's dangerous to create your own kombucha at home.

There are people who believe that kombucha should be prepared in a secured facility, with set temperatures and by trained professionals. Yes, cleanliness is definitely important, but you have to remember that kombucha is antiseptic in itself, hence harmful microorganisms and bacteria won't be able to survive.

As long as you prepare cultured foods such as kombucha properly, then you have low risks of obtaining foodborne illnesses. Once you see mold in your SCOBY, just toss the brew like what you do with moldy fruit, cheese or bread. Educate yourself with safe brewing methods, and you'll be okay.

Kombucha will make you drunk.

Some think kombucha will make you drunk because of its alcohol content. However, the alcohol content in kombucha produced during initial fermentation is just about 0.5% alcohol content, compared to the alcohol content of "light" beer, which is around 3.5 to 4.5%.

Because of the low alcohol content, kombucha is seen as safe even for children. The sugar and caffeine levels are also low – the more kombucha is recommended for anyone. Further fermentations may increase the alcohol content of kombucha, but it still won't reach 3.5%, and won't have as much impact like the usual alcohol drinks.

There are deaths that are caused by kombucha.

This isn't true; there have been no documented deaths related to kombucha tea. Two decades ago, there were unexplained deaths among kombucha drinkers, but soon, it was discovered that kombucha had nothing to do with it.

What kombucha does is to contribute to your good health; it shouldn't make you sick, or worse, lead to your death. As long as you follow good practices in preparing, cooking and preserving kombucha, then you shouldn't have any problems with kombucha itself.

Kombucha can cure all diseases.

Kombucha definitely is a product with lots of health benefits, but it's not a miracle product that can heal all illnesses. What it does is to give back the body's internal balance by improving digestion and by detoxification. Once the body regains its natural internal balance, then the immune system will take over and heal the body.

Kombucha functions as an adaptogen. Adaptogen has three characteristics:

- Nontoxic – it's safe to use,
- Nonspecific – it works on your whole body rather than a single part or system
- Helps the body maintain homeostasis i.e. internal equilibrium.

Kombucha can pretty much help you with any concern you may have on your body, but you have to remember that it's not kombucha itself that does the trick – it only helps your body achieve the goal you wish to attain.

These are just some of the myths surrounding kombucha. There may be kombucha components that aren't scientifically proven, but the fact remains that there are people who swear by the benefits it gives – and what's important is that it helps with the betterment of people's health.

Conclusion

Again, thank you for purchasing this book!

I hope this book was able to help you understand what kombucha is, how to brew it, and what effects drinking kombucha can do to your body.

You might have been a stranger to kombucha before, but now, you're able to prepare kombucha – even from scratch. From simple household ingredients, you can make a probiotic drink that gives you benefits that your whole body will enjoy; after all, almost all ingredients can be found inside your kitchen.

The next step is to apply the steps you've learned in this book. Make your own kombucha that's YOURS – with the taste and aroma you prefer – and soon, you'll reap the benefits of this probiotic drink, and you'll soon wish that you should have learned this earlier.

Don't be afraid to try out making kombucha on your own. As mentioned frequently in this book, as long as you follow the instructions and you take note of all reminders especially regarding cleanliness, then you'll do just fine.

Good luck to you and to your future kombucha creations!

Made in the USA
Middletown, DE
20 December 2020